MAZES ON MARS

written and illustrated

BY **PATRICK MERRELL**

published BY

Troll

DEDICATED

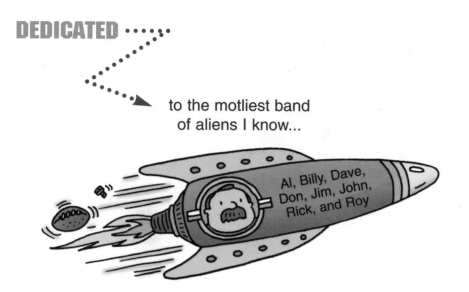

to the motliest band
of aliens I know...

Al, Billy, Dave,
Don, Jim, John,
Rick, and Roy

Panic
broke out in
1719 when Mars
was thought to be
a comet headed
right for
Earth.

This edition published in 2002.

Copyright © 1999 by Patrick Merrell.

Published by Troll Communications L.L.C.

Book design by Patrick Merrell.

ISBN 0-8167-5945-6

Printed in the United States of America.

10 9 8 7 6 5 4 3 2

INTRODUCTION

NASA (the National Aeronautics and Space Administration) has sent probes, orbiters, and landers to explore Mars. They have done a fine job collecting all sorts of information about the planet, but one thing has been sorely lacking—a search for Martian mazes.

You heard me right. My name is Sy Fide, head of MAZE (Master Analyzers of Zigzagging Enigmas). Mazes are everywhere, and it is our goal is to find them wherever they might be. Sounds pretty useless, doesn't it? But think about it. Without MAZE's research there would be no...uh...well, there wouldn't be this book for one thing, and where would that leave you?

Last year, in between NASA missions, we sent our own MAZE lander to Mars to search the planet's surface for mazes. What we found was more than we ever could have hoped for—Mars was crawling with mazes.

Unfortunately, as we soon discovered, the source of most of those mazes was a fleet of motley aliens who were using Mars as a staging area for an invasion of Earth!

I kept a logbook of the events as they unfolded. You will find it—and the Martian mazes we uncovered—on the pages that follow. • • • • • • • • • • • • ▶

TWO DAYS TO LAUNCH... Operation DUMM (Discover Unknown Martian Mazes) nears liftoff. My wife, Clara Fide, puts the finishing touches on the MESS (Maze Exploration Search Satellite), shown below. Before we can launch the MESS, Clara needs to power up its battery. Can you figure out which one of these power cables is actually attached to the MESS?

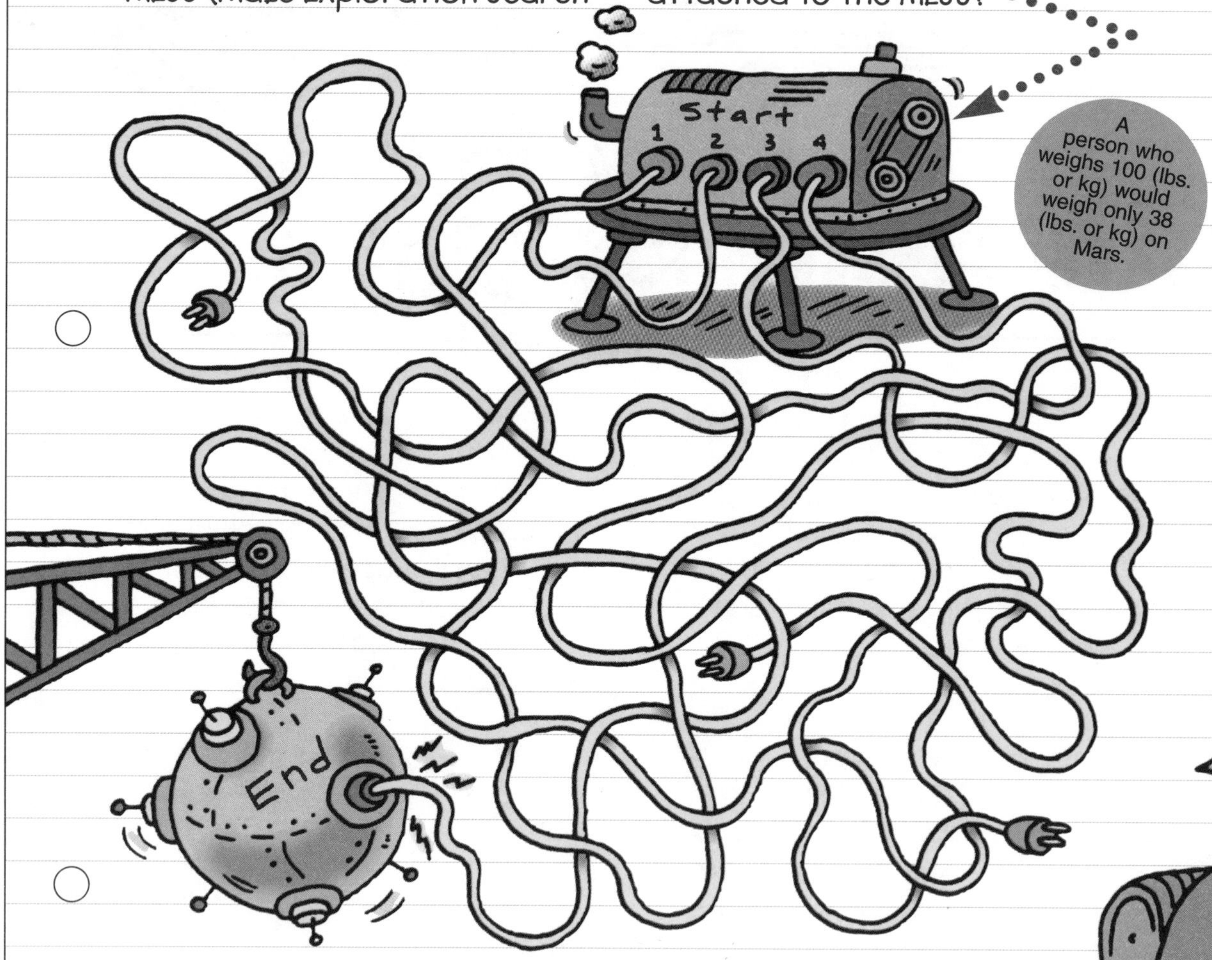

Start
1 2 3 4

End

A person who weighs 100 (lbs. or kg) would weigh only 38 (lbs. or kg) on Mars.

ONE DAY TO LAUNCH...My brother Morty Fide makes the final calculations to plot the route the MAZE satellite will be taking on its trip to Mars. Morty reports the total travel time will be 11 months, 2 days, 3 hours, 16 minutes — or, in Morty time, 912 doughnuts.

On the next page you will see the map Morty has been working on. Unfortunately, Morty tried out many different routes before arriving at the correct one. Can you make some sense of his scrawling and find the route that will take our satellite through the solar system to Mars?

③ VILLA FIDE

ONE MINUTE TO LAUNCH...You may have already noticed that MAZE is a family operation. The truth is, 83 years ago, when my Great Grandmother Mummy Fide first hatched the idea for MAZE, she had a little trouble getting other people interested in it. She was soon forced into plan B — having children, and then grandchildren, in order to staff her dream.

The first MAZE research lab went up in the middle of the family's olive groves. As the Fide family grew, so did the facilities, until there were more buildings (and even more Fides) than olives.

Below, you will see a map of the grounds. As we begin our final countdown, can you find a route from the control tower to the launch platform?

In ancient Rome, the first three days of the week were Sunday, Moon-day & Mars-day.

④ 5..4..3..2..1...

LAUNCH...My father, Dan D. Fide, who is our launch director, goes through the final checklist:

- Batteries.................charged
- MESS...............on launchpad
- Doughnuts............delivered
- Mars...............still out there
- Telemetry.........................huh?

"All systems GO!" Dan finally barks out. "Ignition!" my cousin Vinny barks out. "Woof!" my dog Ratty barks out. A cloud of flame and smoke erupts from under the MESS, the launch platform shakes as a huge "pffft" fills the air, and the MESS slowly lifts into the sky.

On the next page you will see the main control panel that got all this into motion. As you can see, it is an intricate series of switches that must be flipped one after another. Following the arrows, can you find the sequence of switches that gave us liftoff? • • • • • • • • ➤

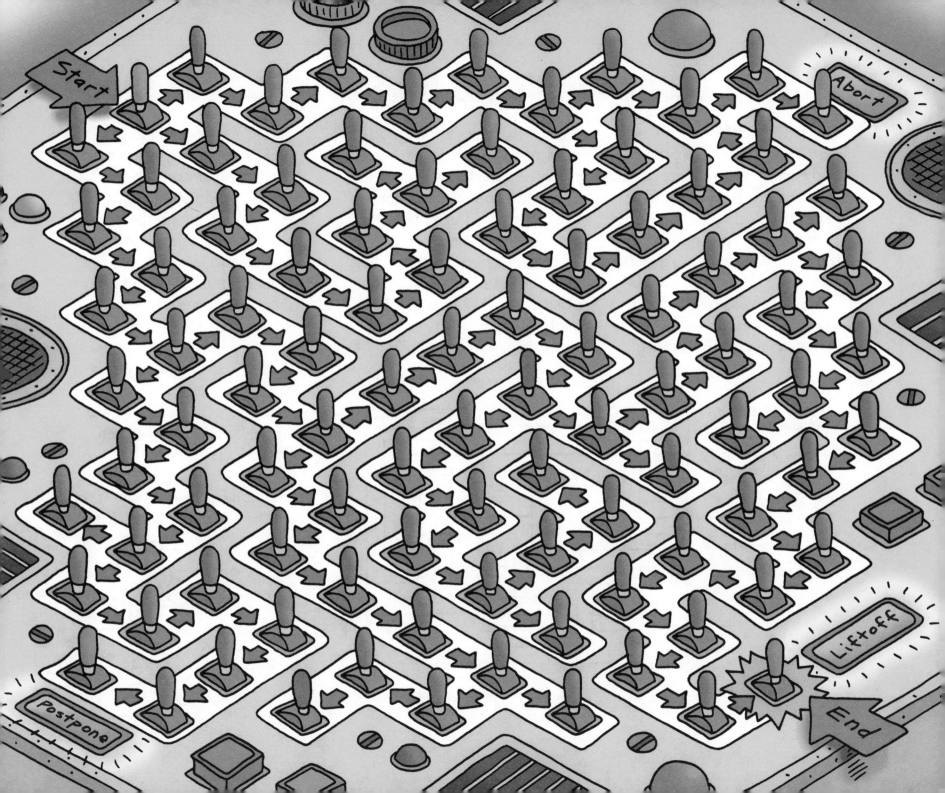

THE TRIP TO MARS…You'll be glad to hear that I'm going to skip right over the long, boring trip that took up the next 11 months, 2 days, 3 hours, and 16 minutes and get right to the much more exciting events on Mars.

Once the MESS began orbiting Mars in preparation for deploying its PLOP (Primary Lander & Observational Pod), my mother, Vera Fide, issued a press release to the media. Only one paper, a supermarket tabloid named the *National Muck*, carried the story.

I include a copy of this article only because the story is positioned next to a puzzle section, which features a maze. (Lucky for us, huh?) • • • • •

ORBIT AROUND MARS…As the MESS nears completion of its first orbit around the red planet, my daughter Misty Fide, who is monitoring the cameras on board, spots something.

"Come take a look at this!" she exclaims. The sight that meets our eyes as we crowd around her chair stops us in our tracks—an enormous fleet of alien spaceships is hovering around the planet!

As you can see on the next page, the ships have been linked together. Starting with the ship farthest from Mars, can you figure out how to get to the ship closest to Mars? • •

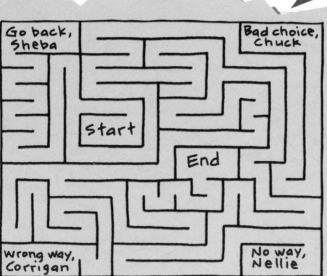

UNI-FIDE FAMILY, CLASSI-FIDE PROJECT

A family with a history of undertaking unusual projects has outdone itself by launching a probe to the planet Mars. The Fides, a one-time olive-growing clan, claim the probe has been sent to collect mazes from the red planet.

"Hogwash!" neighbor Stan Anston says. "They've made this whole thing up to try and sell maze books."

—cont'd. on page 44 —

Go back, Sheba

Bad choice, Chuck

Start

End

Wrong way, Corrigan

No way, Nellie

Mars has two small potato-shaped moons, Phobos and Deimos.

⑦ PLOP DROP　　　　　　⑧ TOP-OGRAPHY

PLOP DEPLOYED...Laser fire from the planet's surface begins to pepper the area around the MESS. My uncle, Terry Fide, immediately orders PLOP deployment.

As the pod plummets through the atmosphere, it must steer a ragged course through a haphazard barrage of laser fire. Can you find a route that will get it safely down? •••••••

Listeners to a 1938 radio broadcast of *War of the Worlds* thought Mars was really attacking Earth.

Start

End

TOUCHDOWN...Petra Fide, my aunt and PLOP system specialist, opens the PLOP's remote-control hatch and raises up the PLOP's TOP (Telescoping Observational Platform). The TOP's cameras are activated, and 12 minutes later (the time it takes radio waves to travel from Mars to Earth) pictures from the planet's surface show us a planet that is teeming with space creatures of all shapes and sizes!

As Petra completes a sweep of the site, she also discovers a large city the aliens have built. It is a confusing jumble of building units and connecting tubes. We haved dubbed it the EECH (Extraterrestrial Environmentally Controlled Habitat).

Traveling through the buildings and tubes, can you find a way to get to the aliens' movie theater? •••••••

COW ACTIVATION...My nephew, Cody Fide, needs to send a signal to the PLOP's BARN (Battery-Activated Rover Nest) to begin powering up the COW (Computer-Operated Wanderer).

Once powered, the COW will venture out and explore the planet. But first, Cody must send a code word to allow the unit to start up. To find out what the code word is, you will need to decode the symbols below. Follow each symbol to find out what letter it stands for. Write the letters in the blank spaces as you get each one. • • • • • • • • • • • • • • •

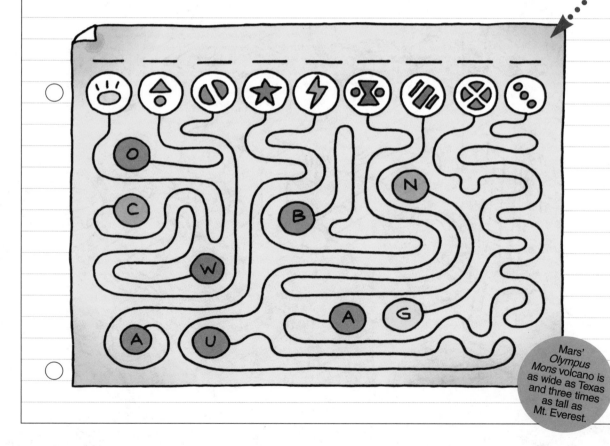

Mars' Olympus Mons volcano is as wide as Texas and three times as tall as Mt. Everest.

Here's the situation up to this point: MAZE gets project DUMM off the ground by launching a MESS. Having reached Mars, MAZE's DUMM MESS drops its PLOP, pops its TOP, and lets the COW out of the BARN. And we're still not even halfway through! EECH!

AND THEN...My niece, Tippy Fide, reports an unusual sighting from the COW. The COW lenses reveal a large crater field filled with tunnels the aliens have been digging. Sir T. Fide, a distant English relative and an expert in ODD (Otherworldly Deportment and Demeanor), examines the situation.

"The aliens have labeled the craters with letters," Sir T. declares. "Craters with the same letter are linked by tunnels. By following the paths above ground and the tunnels below ground, these aliens can cross this field."

Can you figure out how? • • • •

⑪ HERE, ROVER

ROVER RENDEZVOUS… What we discover next is something even more unexpected than the aliens. My sister Bonnie Fide is the first to notice it—a set of tread tracks crisscrossing the planet's surface. As she studies the tracks, she soon finds the source—the *Sojourner* rover from NASA's *Pathfinder* mission!

You may remember this mission. On July 4, 1997, the *Pathfinder* lander set down on Mars. Soon after, the *Sojourner* rover ventured out to examine the Martian rocks. After three months, *Sojourner* was never heard from again.

Until now! Not only is *Sojourner* still operating, but it has made quite a maze of tracks for us. Starting at the lander, can you find the path that leads to the rover? •••••

A Martian year lasts 687 Earth days (almost two years).

If you lived on Mars, you would be only about half as many years old.

Russia's *Mars 3* capsule sent 20 seconds of pictures from the surface of Mars in 1971.

SPACE RACE
MAZE GAME

FIRST EVENING… The Martian day is almost the same length as ours (24 hours, 37 minutes, 23 seconds). As evening approaches, the COW observes an unusual activity going on. The aliens are playing a game.

After printing out a picture of the game board taken by COW's cameras, we consult with our top expert in game design— my other daughter, Glora Fide.

Glora examines the board and figures out how the game is played. Here are the rules:

1. Any number of players can play. Each player needs to find a playing piece.
2. Start at "START" and take turns. Each player flips a coin to move. Follow the "heads" or "tails" arrow. Only one coin flip per turn!
3. Follow any directions of the space you land on. (Two pieces can be on the same space at the same time.)
4. Aim for Mars. When you get to Mars, shift your playing piece to the next page. Now head for Earth. First one to Earth wins. •••►

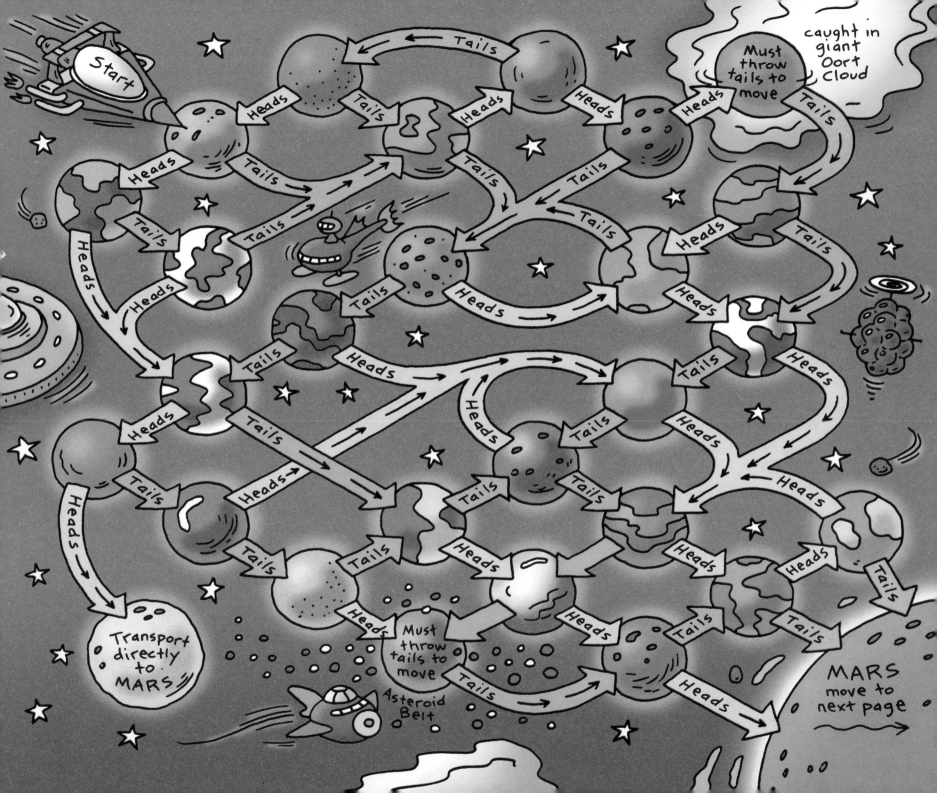

⑫ NECK AND NECK...AND NECK... ⑬ EERIE EVENTS

DAY TWO ON MARS...As the sun rises and warms the planet from a chilly -100°F (-76°C) up to +7°F (-14°C), we are jolted awake by the sight of a hideous space creature filling the screens of our monitors.

My younger sister, Sissy Fide, a trained alienologist, examines the structure of this thing. She begins by trying to trace the path from the creature's body to its purple head. Can you help her? • • • • • • • • • •

STILL DAY TWO ON MARS... As we begin to monitor the planet more closely, it becomes obvious that the aliens are up to something. My Grandfather Stu P. Fide extends the EARS (Extraterrestrial Auditory Radar System) to hear what they are saying.

"Mubs ig fribble ketzl quag!" a large green one says. Stu enters this into the WHAT (Word-Hunting Alien Translator).

"Our plans to invade Earth are set!" comes out the translation.

"Yippee!" a squat, spotted alien exclaims.

"Yippee," the translator tells us.

"INVASION!?" we all scream.

While we panic, can you figure out how a word travels through the WHAT and comes out as a translation? • • • • • •➤

Earth is about twice the size of Mars and about ten times heavier.

End ◄ • • • • • •

Start here

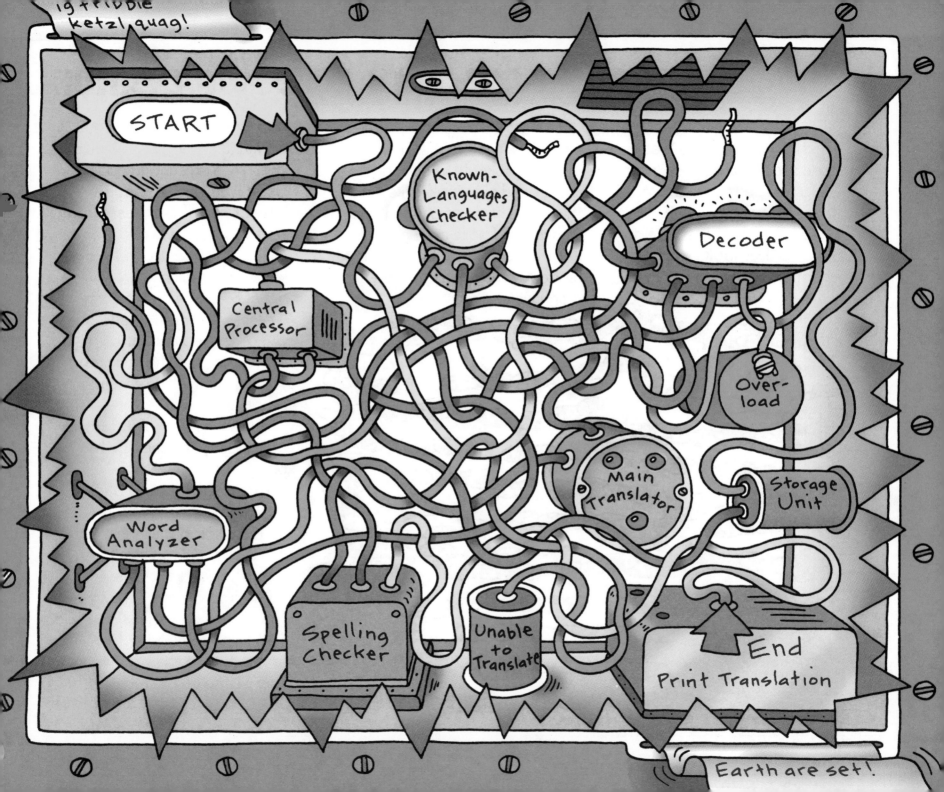

YET STILL DAY TWO ON MARS... "Here, try some of my fresh-baked cookies," my grandmother Molly Fide says in an attempt to calm everyone down.

"Yaaagh!" Aunt Petra yells. "The cookies look just like that squat, spotted alien!"

As she runs screaming from the room, she knocks Grandma Molly's cookie tray, sending the baked alien look-alikes flying to the ground. They land in a jumbled maze on the floor.

Perhaps it would be best to solve it while we try to collect ourselves. • • • • • • • • • • • • • • •

AND EVEN MORE OF DAY TWO ON MARS..."Hey, take a look at this," says my second cousin, Ossie Fide, one of the real backbones of our operation. On the screen, we see the aliens grouped around the large green alien. We nickname him ALGA (short for A Large Green Alien). ALGA is giving the others some sort of instruction, and hanging next to him is something resembling a mobile.

"But it's not a mobile," Ossie concludes. "It's their battle plan for invading Earth!" Ossie points out that each of the hanging pieces represents one of the ships in their fleet. "This is a 3-D model of their flying formation," he explains.

It is also a maze. Following the strings and sticks, can you find a route from the main ship at the top to the Vaporizing Ship at the bottom?• • •
• • • • •

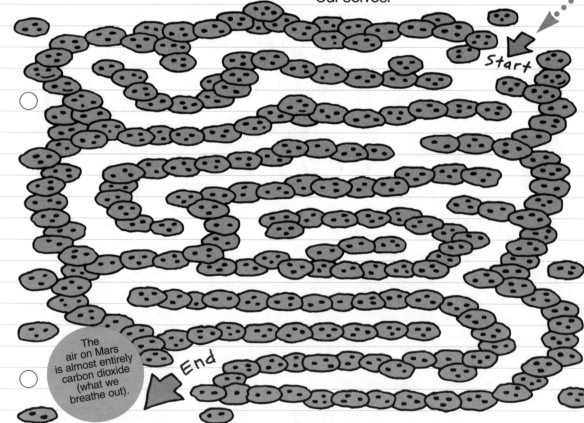

Start

End

The air on Mars is almost entirely carbon dioxide (what we breathe out).

LATER THAT DAY…Keeping a close eye on ALGA, my sister-in-law, Electra Fide, notices that the pattern on his legs is a maze. Starting with the tentacle on the right, can you find a path to the end of the tentacle on the left?

Billions of years ago there were floods and active volcanoes on Mars.

End

Start

THAT EVENING…The sun begins to set. As the temperature drops, the aliens head toward their sleeping quarters in the EECH, just on the other side of a dried-up riverbed. The "canals" in this bed were formed by water long ago when the atmosphere on Mars was more like Earth's.

Winding your way through the riverbed, can you get the aliens to the EECH?

Canals, thought to be water-carrying ditches dug by Martians, were first sighted in 1877.

In 1965, pictures taken by *Mariner 4* proved that there are no canals on Mars.

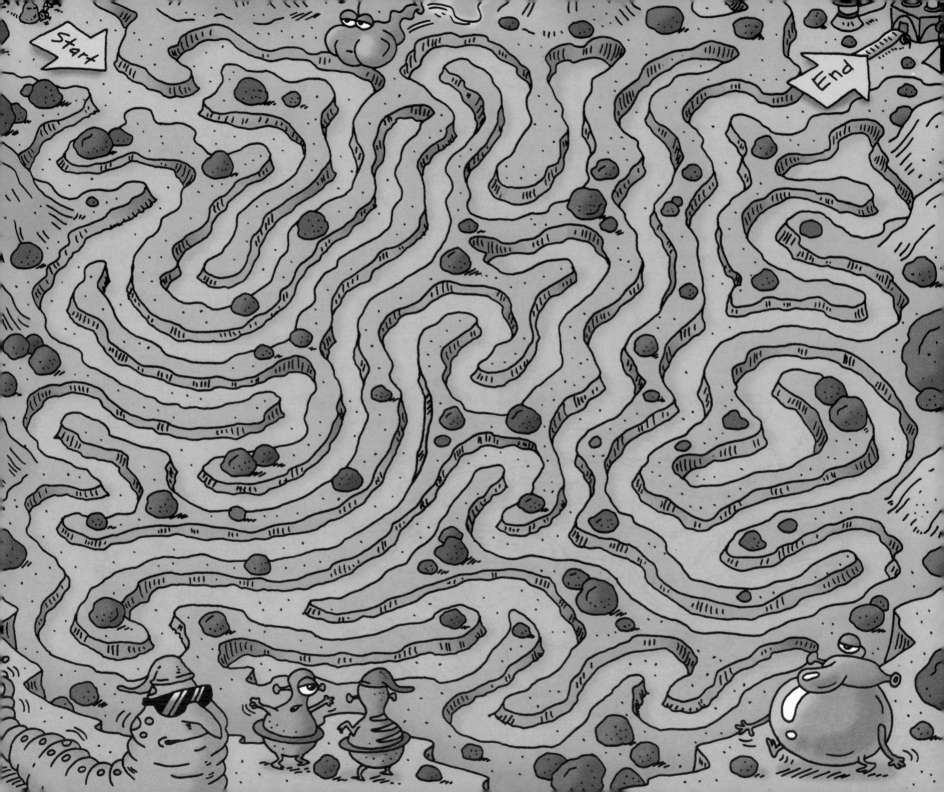

⑱ ROPE A SCOPE

DAY THREE ON MARS... We arise on the third day of our odyssey with a feeling of dread. "We're doomed," my son Horry Fide grumbles. "It's hopeless," his twin, Rary Fide, agrees. (Their names were supposed to be Harry and Rory, until a hospital clerk fouled up the spelling on their birth certificates.)

The rest of us agree there seems little we can do to stop the impending invasion. We helplessly watch as ALGA and his minions begin assembling a giant telescope to check out their route to Earth.

Below, you will see boxes of parts being towed to the site. Can you figure out which alien is pulling which box? • • • • •

When Mars is at its closest to Earth, it is one of the most visible objects in our sky.

⑲ HOPE?

FOUR HOURS LATER... It took them quite a while, but the aliens have finally gotten their telescope put together. My youngest brother, Eddie Fide, tries to raise our spirits by pointing out what a botched job they have made of it.

"Look at that thing," Eddie chuckles. "Half the tubes on it are useless. It's just a big mess!" As we listen through EARS, however, it is obvious that the telescope does work.

"Wargo pilsits fod!" ALGA says as he looks through the eyepiece. ("I see something.")... "Quom martley." ("It's made of metal.")..."Foz gotta minno." ("Something's written on it.")... "EGAD! Gobsly hifto eeby Nasa wada Grud!" ("Egad! It's been sent by our sworn enemy — Nasa of the planet Grud!")

We're all very confused. While we try to sort this out, can you figure out how ALGA sees through this thing? • • • • • •

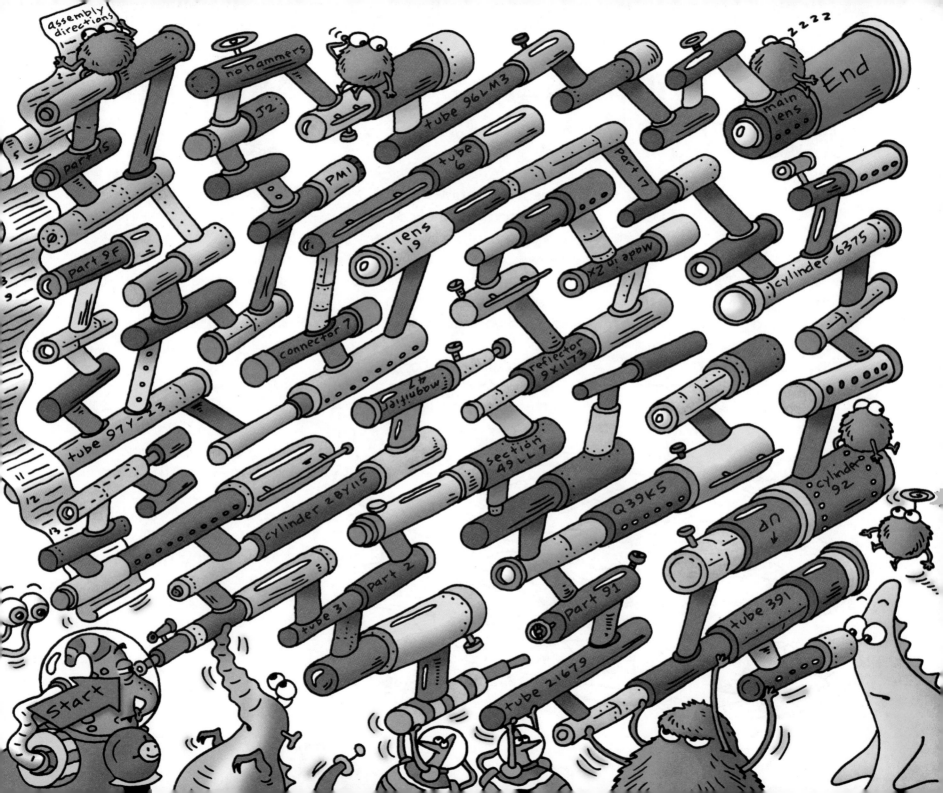

⑳ RETREAT!

AFTERNOON OF THE THIRD DAY ON MARS… As we watch the alien force run around in a state of panic, my great aunt, Dee Fide, offers an explanation.

"First of all," she says, "what the aliens saw is a NASA spacecraft—it's on its way to explore Mars. Second, from what we can make of the aliens' yelling and screaming, they seem to have a powerful enemy who has been chasing them around the galaxy. And get this—his name is Nasa!

They think that NASA's ship is Nasa's ship!"

"Chalk one up for our side!" my great uncle, Cal C. Fide, exclaims, and the whole control room erupts into a big cheer. While we celebrate, the aliens continue their frantic scramble to evacuate the planet. Their ships land and ramps are extended.

Starting at the end of the ramps, can you figure out which ramp leads to which ship? • • • • • • • • • •

㉑ STAR ROUTE

THE END… Mars is soon empty, with no trace that the alien force has ever even been there. We are a little disappointed that the approaching NASA spacecraft won't be able to document what we have all just witnessed. On the other hand, we are glad that the motley invaders are gone and heading at top speed away from Earth.

My stepsister, Vivvy Fide, activates the FOOT (Far-Off Observation Telescope) aboard the MESS, which is still orbiting Mars. The alien route zigs, backtracks, and zags as they make their way out of the solar system. We assume this is to avoid being followed by Nasa!

We create a map of the route using DIRT (Direct Imaging Route Tracker). Starting at Mars, and traveling only in the direction of the arrows, can you find the route to their ships? • • • • • • ▶

Most stars were named by Arab astronomers and scholars during the Middle Ages.

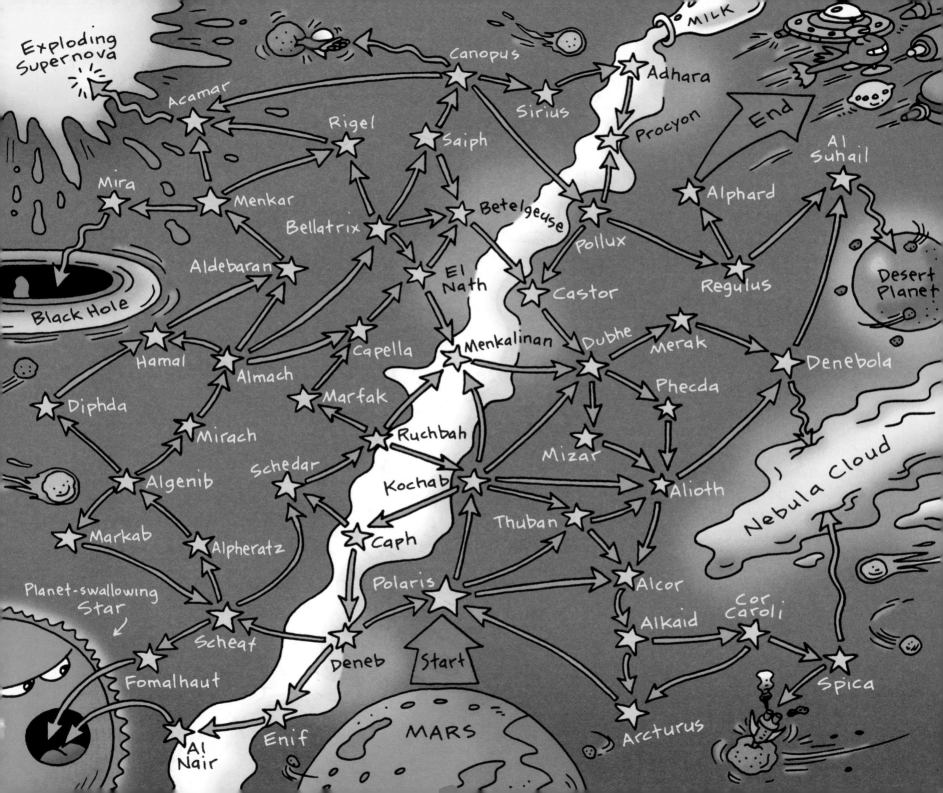

㉒ BOOK END

ONE YEAR LATER...You probably thought that was the end of it, didn't you? Well, it was, except for one last thing—getting a publisher to print this story! Let me tell you, it's not easy when this is what you've got...

"Well, it's about an organization named MAZE and their DUMM project to send a MESS to Mars. The MESS's PLOP spots aliens from its TOP. An ODD relative watches as the COW is let out of the BARN and then, using its EARS and our WHAT, uncovers ALGA's plan to invade Earth! Lucky for us, NASA, but not the Nasa that ALGA thinks, scares them off. The alien's retreat is tracked by FOOT, and then drawn using DIRT."

Amazingly, a publisher went for it! Can you find the route that brought me to this fine company?

THE ANSWERS

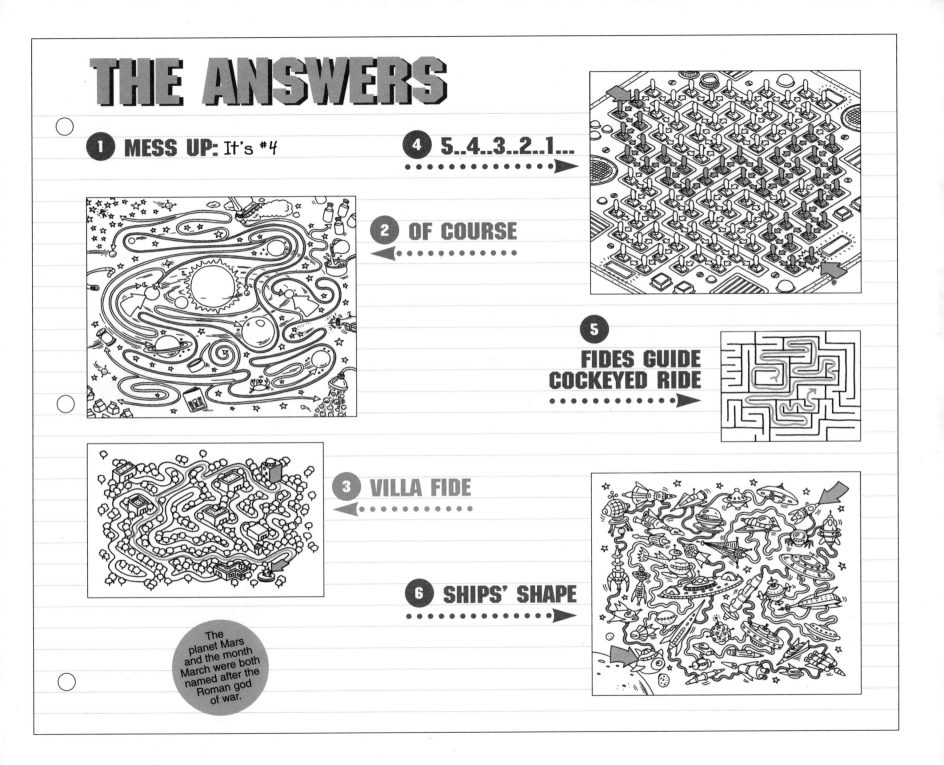

1 **MESS UP:** It's #4

2 **OF COURSE** ●●●●●●●●●●◄

3 **VILLA FIDE** ●●●●●●●●●◄

4 **5..4..3..2..1...** ●●●●●●●●●●●●►

5 **FIDES GUIDE COCKEYED RIDE** ●●●●●●●●●●●►

6 **SHIPS' SHAPE** ●●●●●●●●●●●●►

The planet Mars and the month March were both named after the Roman god of war.

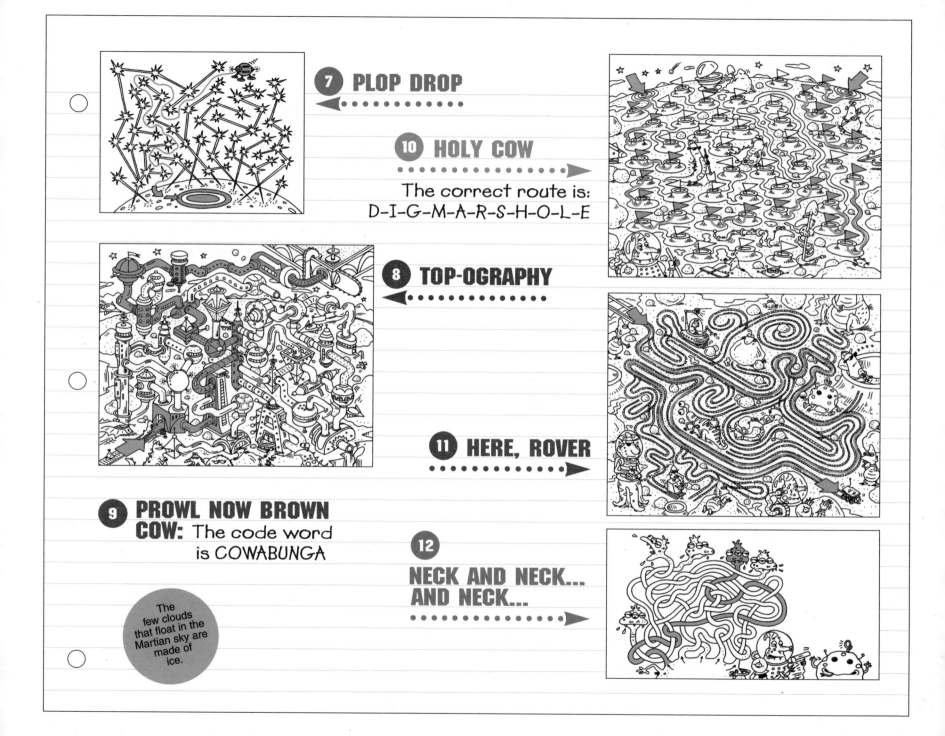

7 PLOP DROP

10 HOLY COW

The correct route is:
D–I–G–M–A–R–S–H–O–L–E

8 TOP-OGRAPHY

11 HERE, ROVER

9 PROWL NOW BROWN COW: The code word is COWABUNGA

The few clouds that float in the Martian sky are made of ice.

12 NECK AND NECK... AND NECK...

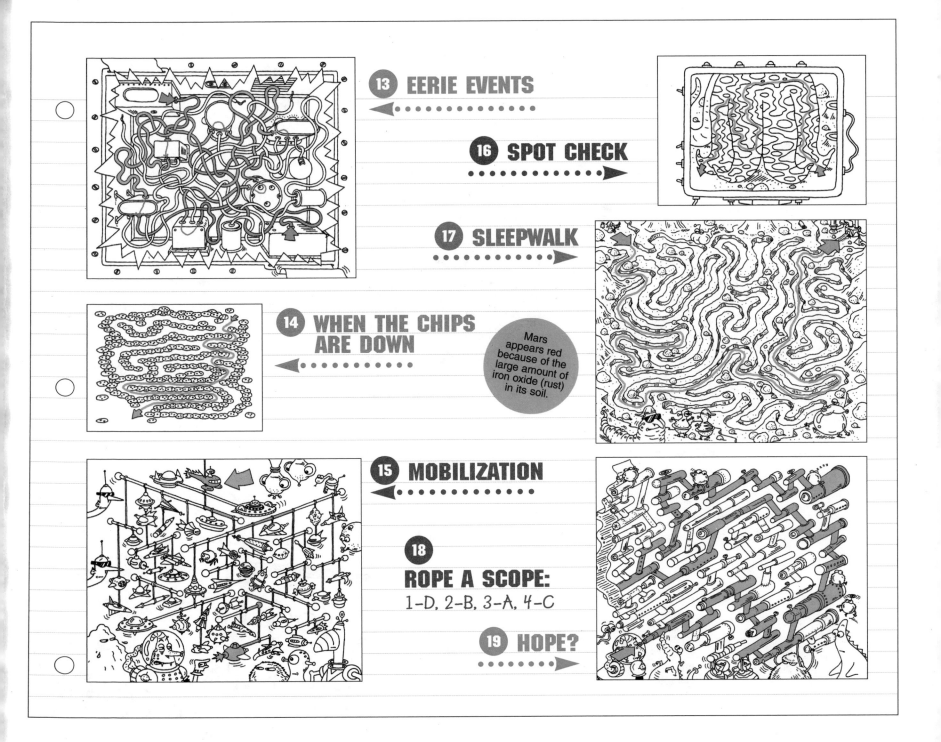

13 EERIE EVENTS

16 SPOT CHECK

17 SLEEPWALK

14 WHEN THE CHIPS ARE DOWN

Mars appears red because of the large amount of iron oxide (rust) in its soil.

15 MOBILIZATION

18
ROPE A SCOPE:
1-D, 2-B, 3-A, 4-C

19 HOPE?

20 RETREAT!: 1-A, 2-B, 3-C

21 STAR ROUTE ••••••

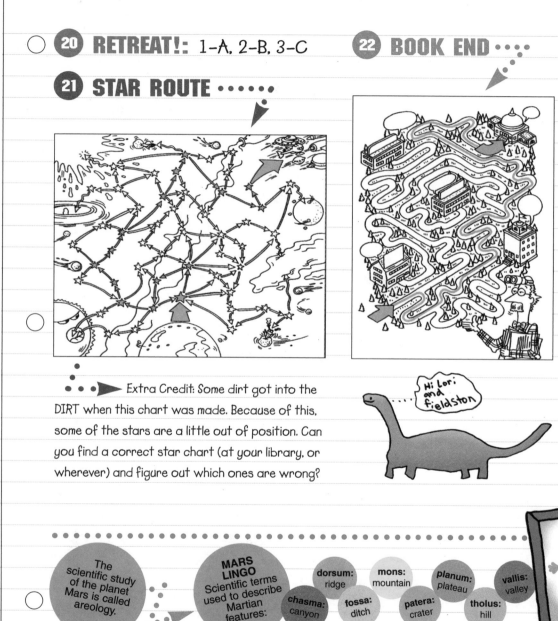

► Extra Credit: Some dirt got into the DIRT when this chart was made. Because of this, some of the stars are a little out of position. Can you find a correct star chart (at your library, or wherever) and figure out which ones are wrong?

22 BOOK END ••••

Hi Lori and fieldston

ABOUT THE AUTHOR

Even though I, Sy Fide, am the sole creator of MAZES ON MARS, it has come to my attention that Patrick Merrell is claiming to have had something to do with this book. This undeserving usurper, who lives in Mount Vernon, NY, with his wife, Mary Dee, and daughter, Jamie, has created many other literary masterpieces (such as the mesmerizing MAZE★MANIA, the mind-boggling MASTERMIND MAZES, the menacing MONSTER MAZES, the diabolical DOUBLECROSS MAZES, and the perplexing PUZZLED PENGUINS). But his closest connection to this book is having once eaten a Mars candy bar, which he probably pilfered as well.

The scientific study of the planet Mars is called areology.

MARS LINGO Scientific terms used to describe Martian features:

chasma: canyon

dorsum: ridge

fossa: ditch

mons: mountain

patera: crater

planum: plateau

tholus: hill

vallis: valley